# Do You Admit to Not Making Love on Your Wedding Night?

# Other books by Barry Sinrod

*The First Really Important Survey of American Habits*
(with Mel Poretz)

*The Baby Name Personality Survey*
(with Bruce Lansky)

*Do You Do It With The Lights On?*
(With Mel Poretz)

*Do You Do It When Your Pets Are In The Room?*

*Just Married*
(with Marlo Grey)

*The Baby Name Survey*
(with Bruce Lansky)

*The Do You Series*

# Do You Admit to Not Making Love on Your Wedding Night?

*A Look Into the Private Lives of Newlyweds of All Ages*

Barry Sinrod
and
Marlo Mittler

SelectBooks, Inc.
New York

Do You Admit to Not Making Love on Your Wedding Night?
Copyright © 2002 by Barry Sinrod and Marlo Mittler.

This edition published by SelectBooks, Inc. For information address
SelectBooks, Inc., New York, New York.

First Edition

ISBN 1-59079-000-6

Library of Congress Cataloging-in-Publication Data
Sinrod, Barry and Mittler, Marlo
Do You Admit to Not Making Love on Your Wedding Night?-1st ed.

Manufactured in the United States of America

10 9 8 7 6 5 4 3 2 1

# Contents

# Dedications and Acknowledgments

Barry's:

I dedicate this book to both "newlyweds" and "old married people like me" all over the world. This is the first in what we hope is a never ending series of books under the umbrella title Do you? I want to thank Kenzi Sugihara of Select Books? For helping to develop the idea and for his faith in all of the work that I have done previously. Without him there would be no "Do You" series.

All of you that read this book will see that love and marriage must be worked at every day, whether you are married one day or 40 years. Our book looks at the light side of marriage and takes a peek at the things we take for granted. It will also provide you with an inside view to see if you and your spouse match up to what the American Public told us. In other words, this book is for those who have only recently been married as well as those who have been married for 50 years, married a second time, have no children, small children, grown children, married children, grandchildren.

Of course, I give extra special recognition to my life, my love, my everything, my bride of nearly 40 years and still the sexiest of them all, my wife, Shelly.

To my wonderful children, their spouses and my six grandchildren I thank them all for standing by me and being the inspiration for this book, I love them all very very much. My thanks to my wonderful daughter-in-law Felice Sinrod for her great work in setting up and doing the wonderful graphics in this book. Thanks Felice, I love you!

Marlo's:
I dedicate this book to those special married folks around me:

My parents for truly showing me how wonderful marriage can be and how love between two people can conquer all.

My sister and brother-in-law for paving the road and showing me how commitment and trust, humor and love makes a marriage strong and exciting.

My brother and sister-in-law for reminding me how much fun being newlyweds truly is!

My friends for sharing with me their own secrets, remedies, tales, anecdotes and joys of making a marriage successful.

To my own husband, my love at first sight, my "bechert," my everything.

And, lastly, to my kids, I look forward to the day when you, too, will enjoy the wonderful world of marriage!

# Introduction

When my daughter (Marlo) and I spoke to and met with several publishers we met Kenzi Sugihara who took a look at all of our previous works and came up with the idea for a series of Do You books we knew this is where we wanted to be.

To start the Do You series, we decided to revisit some of the subjects we had written about before. We added new questions and went back and asked some of the same questions again (some as far back at 15 years ago) to get the most up to date answers.

This first book came about as a result of the three wonderful weddings that my wife and I have had the privilege of making and since they cost us so much money, we are hoping that lots of people will buy this book!

So many great, funny and poignant things came out of the wedding experience that I decided to invite my daughter Marlo to come along for this ride and help me write this book.

We know that you will enjoy it very much, it will make you think, laugh and cry and just have some plain old fun. Enjoy it and tell your friends about it. We would welcome any comments on anything in the book. Simply send them to http://www.allaboutdoyou.com.

# The Facts

What a world we live in! With 21st technology we were able to write this entire book utilizing the internet. We were able to find 4,254 newlyweds of all ages. These people have been married from one day to two years and they reside in all 50 states, urban, suburban, rural and they are of all races.

A questionnaire was sent via the internet to people who had registered as a possible recipient of a research questionnaire.

We never ever asked for their names. The questions as you will see are very private, everything goes, no holds barred! Having been a marketing researcher for nearly 40 years it is imperative that we give complete privacy to each and every respondent. The individual names are never ever an issue, only the answers to the questions which appear in the book. Certain demographics are asked so that we can classify people by age, income, geography, etc.

All of this adds up to a great time! We are confident that these people told us the truth, because as mentioned no names attached anywhere. The statistical margin of error is plus or minus 3 percent!

Are you ready to see where you stand or should stand or might stand? This book will take you on a wonderful ride, from the day a couple meets through the first two years of marriage. Whether you are a newlywed at age 18 or 93 or have been married for 20 or 40 years you will enjoy this book as you compare what you have done, will do or are doing now.

Everyone has told us over the years that the thing they like most about our books is that they are a great coffee table, bathroom and conversation piece that brings out the best and sometimes the worst of someone as they discuss what is inside this book.

It is a great gift for the newlywed to be as well as those who are nearing an anniversary.

So sit back and relax and have a great time!

# Chapter 1

They meet, they fall in love
They take the next steps...
towards the altar

# How did you and your spouse first meet?

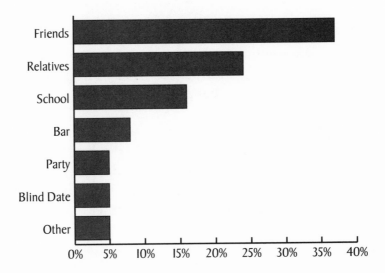

Marlo said: You are going to meet your spouse through introduction either by a friend or relative (including blind dates), according to our newlyweds. I met my own husband on a blind date. I have since married off two other couples in this manner. Most of my friends met through introductions as well.

Barry said: My date with destiny was a blind date, set up by some mutual friends. It was a few telephone conversations and love at first sight over three weeks that led me to my wife.

# Samples of the ways that people first met:

I met my husband while working at a part-time job. He was a fellow worker who was the height of "grunge". But somehow after many many months I found I couldn't keep him out of my mind and so I made a move and the rest is history.

Our parents met each on their honeymoon and remained casual friends for more than 25 years, when suddenly I opened my eyes and realized that their daughter who I had known all my life was a beautiful, sexy, woman. Hello, we fell love after not even looking at each other in that way for 21 years.

I met her in class at school. I asked her out, and on our first date, she brought along a friend. Two weeks later I asked her to marry me.

I was her mother's waiter in the Catskill mounatins. Her mother fell in love with me, introduced us and soon her daughter took the hint. Now we are happily married.

We met at church when we were both 3 years old.

I saw him on The Oprah Winfrey Show, and called the station immediately.

He fell on me at the mall.

First day of college, first day ever away from home. I get to registration and the guy behind the desk asks me if I want a locker and to pick a number. I tell him # 69. I had always heard people laugh at that number but had no idea what it meant. Needless to say, I soon found out when everyone laughed at me, especially the guys. Surprisingly, the guy behind the desk called me at my dorm anyway, and from that day on we were never apart.

My son's social circle was included a large number of male and female friends. One night, he came home to us and said there is one girl that he would really like to ask out on a "real date." He said, "What should I do? What if she says no, or if it doesn't work out, I don't want to lose her as my friend, in any event." We told him to go with his heart and believe in fate. He asked her out, she said yes, and soon thereafter, love set in. They married exactly a year later. A real Harry met Sally story.

My older daughter met her husband when they were only 14 and 17, respectively. Their grandparents lived next door to each other in Florida, and they met while the families were on vacation. They continued to date briefly once our family returned home to New York, but lost touch because of their age difference. Nearly six years later, my daughter ran into his brother at a dance club and shortly thereafter she "re-met" her husband-to-be. It was love at second (more mature) sight; she was 20 and he 23 and they married two years later. They now have three of the most beautiful children in the world and soon will be celebrating their 15th wedding anniversary.

Our teenage sons, who are good friends, fixed us up.

We met at someone else's wedding.

I saw her at the food market and then at a drugstore and within one hour I asked her out.

We were both coming out of the bathrooms at an Ohio Turnpike rest stop, and I ran straight into him, knocking him to the floor.

At the bowling alley, he dropped a ball on his foot and needed first aid. I am a nurse.

At college, we were kidding around and he droppedme on my head. Feeling bad, he took me out to dinner.

He saw me getting out of my RX-7. I was wearing skintight pants, and he said it was love at first sight.

He caught a ball at a baseball game and spilled his beer all over me.

We were in a bereavement group.

We met at a baby shower.

We were walking our dogs.

I delivered a pizza to him.

He gave me golf lessons.

# Did you kiss on the first date? Did you sleep together on the first date?

Ok, think we could find something strange from the answers to these rather simple two questions? Well we did... first a few tidbits:

For whatever reason more men (86 percent vs. 72 percent) than women said they kissed good night after their first date, while more women (32 percent vs. 12 percent) said they ended the evening with a very intimate touch. This means that 20 percent of women made love with her guy but he was not aware of it!

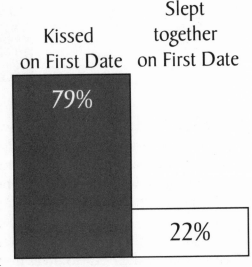

Kissed on First Date — 79%

Slept together on First Date — 22%

But the strangest statistic is that while 22 percent of our couples said they made love on that first date. 11 percent said they made love but didn't kiss!!!

# Love at first sight for either or both of you?

| | YES | NO |
|---|---|---|
| Men | 42% | 58% |
| Women | 56% | 44% |
| Total | 49% | 51% |

Marlo said: Not a surprise to me! It was love at first sight for me, while it took my husband slightly longer. I think I read somewhere that women know in about 5 minutes while it takes men days, weeks, months! They say women fall in love first, but men fall deeper.

Barry said: I was 18 years old when I first met my wife. When I came to the door to meet her for the first time, she said hello and went back inside to get her jacket and she insists she told her mother "this is going to be my husband." It was the furthest thing from my mind at the time, but, it wasn't long that she cajoled me into saying the "L" word. We were engaged 30 days later! Now nearly 40 years have passed and I love her much more than she can possibly love me.

The moral of these two incidences is that you must give love a chance! As you can see from the statistics more than half of the total respondents told us it was NOT love at first sight.

8

# How long did you go together before you first made love?

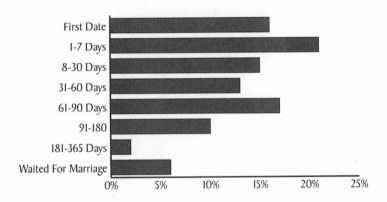

Barry said: This is one of those generation gap questions, one which I surely would not ever discuss with my daughter, but maybe with my son. Since I am from from the old old old school, I admit to the double standard, men vs. women. No letters please. As the FATHER, I find it most interesting that the women are the more aggressive, since more than twice as many women admit to love making on the first date (11% to 5%). Wow! Half of the couples slept together before the first month was over. In our day, we were among the 6% who didn't make (full and complete) love until we were married!

Marlo said: The information we gathered does, in fact, indicate that 82% of my peer group do, in fact, make love before three months have passed. While I realize that it is the 21st century where anything goes, I was still surprised so many people made love before 3 months! I would imagine this trend will go down, or at least I hope so before my kids grow up.

Finally some inside tidbits. If you live in California, New York, South Dakota, Wyoming and Florida you have the best chance of making love on your first date. If you live in Michigan, Indiana, Kentucky or Alabama you might as well get used to waiting at least 93 days!

# How long did you go together before getting engaged?

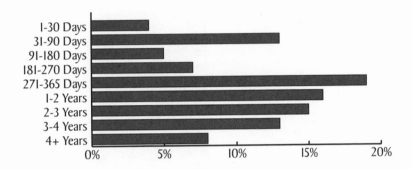

| | |
|---|---|
| 1-30 Days | |
| 31-90 Days | |
| 91-180 Days | |
| 181-270 Days | |
| 271-365 Days | |
| 1-2 Years | |
| 2-3 Years | |
| 3-4 Years | |
| 4+ Years | |

0%    5%    10%    15%    20%

Decide quickly when you find that "true love," as did nearly 1/2 of our couples who got engaged within a year.

If you are waiting and waiting and waiting for the "E" word, and it doesn't happen within 365 days, it seems you will be in it for the long haul.

Those who didn't get engaged within a year waited an average of 1,029 days more (a total of 3.8 years). Perhaps you had better let your companion know there just might be an expiration date without an upcoming engagement date.

# Did he ask for permission to marry you?

YES            NO

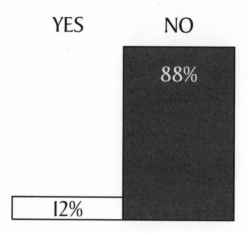

88%

12%

Marlo said: I actually told him early on, don't ask my parents, I wanted to be the one to surprise them! As for my peers, many friends felt asking permission might not always end in a "green light," so they've opted not to ask!

Barry said: I didn't ask for permission nearly 40 years ago, mainly because I was afraid, as I had only known my future wife for less than 30 days. If I were her parents I would have said NO to me, so I took the "chicken" way out and let her tell them. Somehow it has worked out and, in a senior moment, I agree with my daughter. Today, the family is generally not what it was so many years ago, and so if a couple loves each other, there is little a parent can or should do to stop it.

# Who proposed?
# Proposed on bended knee?

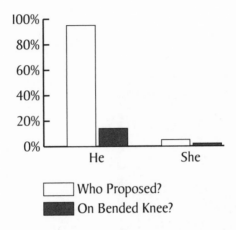

100%
80%
60%
40%
20%
0%

He          She

☐ Who Proposed?
■ On Bended Knee?

Marlo said: Who are the 5 percent of women who actually proposed to their husband to be? Are they crazy? And can you believe that 2 percent of the women actually proposed on bended knee? I don't know any of these women personally, that's for sure.

Barry said: I am surprised that only 95 percent of the men proposed. I would think that it is impossible to get married without that first step by the man, yet 5 percent of the women told us that they were the ones that proposed. 21st century stuff I guess? Bended knees went out with knickers in the 19th century and yet 16 percent of our couples performed that duty. I would have liked to see the 2 percent of women who did it!

13

# Were you ready to accept THE proposal when it came?

YES  NO

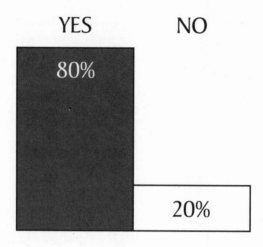

80%

20%

Suprise!  Nearly every new bride to be was ready when they received the all important commitment. While every one of them accepted it was still a surprise at the "very moment" that it happened because the wonderful guy in their life planned it that way.

However, 80 percent of our newly-weds were indeed ready, willing and able and waiting for those important words "Will you marry me?"

# Ok girl, tell us all about that engagement ring!

Did not give her a ring    Did not buy her a diamond

18%

11%

Barry said: I don't quite know what to make of the 18 percent of the men who DID not present ANY kind of ring at the time of the engagement. Furthermore, the 11 percent that didn't buy a diamond.

Marlo said: If I didn't get a ring, and a diamond ring at that, I would have some doubts. After all, it is certainly true that diamonds are a girl's best friend. Seriously, I believe that unless you can't afford even the simplist of rings, it is the only way to do it right.

The all important statistics: We are, of course, very happy that they got a resounding yes anyway, but for the vast majority, diamonds are indeed the gem of choice!

It is interesting that the older group of men (40+) were the most likely not to give a ring. You would think these gentlemen would be wiser and be more financially settled, however, that was not the case.

# Does size really matter?

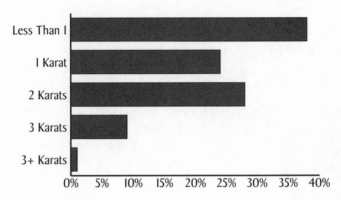

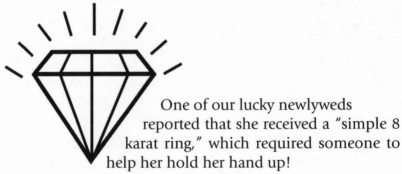

One of our lucky newlyweds reported that she received a "simple 8 karat ring," which required someone to help her hold her hand up!

The average amount spent on purchasing the engagement ring by our wonderful guys was $5,655.00!

Money, Money, Money: Only 19 percent of the men had to borrow money to buy the ring. These guys tended to be the big shots who were older (40+) and richer (over $75K). The need to borrow was probably because they were the ones most likely to try to impress their brides-to-be with one of those 3, 4 or even 8 karat rings.

# Chapter 2

## Leading up to the big day: the honeymoon and getting used to each other

# THE BIG DAY

Nerves were shot, frazzled and out of control! The person who was most responsible for that during the planning of the wedding day was:

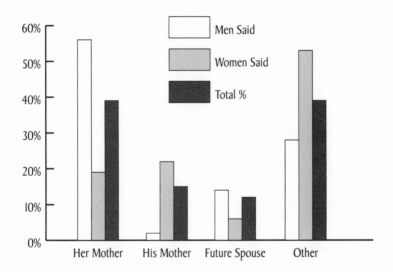

Barry said: Could it be any clearer! Is it no wonder that us men are driven crazy right from the beginning. The answers to this question show that it is the women who put our nerves to the test. How can we ever win, when we are up against our future wife, her mother, and every one of her female relatives and friends, who are all there with advise.

Marlo said: I see nothing wrong with the numbers above. It is only us "real ladies" that want to be sure that THE DAY is perfect. The men don't seem to care as much.

Presssure, much like Billy Joel sings in one of his many hits...

# Did you feel it day after day as you came closer to the big day?

(If yes, were you ever thinking of calling the whole thing off?)

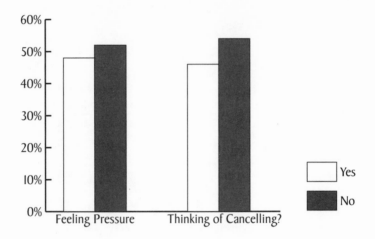

Marlo said: What would a great wedding be like without pressure, nerves, nerves, arguing, money, your mother, your mother-in-law, everyone you ever knew in your life and even those you don't know? "Anticipation," Carly Simon's song, is more like it than Billy Joel's "Pressure." Like most things, the "Anticipation" is much worse than the actual circumstance. We had our share of it, but all that mattered was that it turned out to be the most perfect wedding day a girl could dream of!

Barry said: My nerves were completely shot because I was shelling out the money by the hour and couldn't wait for it to stop. I didn't know if I would make it down the stretch. I see that nearly half (46 percent) of our couples said they were thinking of calling it off because of all the pressure. If my daughter and son-in-law-to-be had tried calling it off after I had so much time and money invested in it, I would have gone crazy! I sure can understand how people can be driven to insanity while preparing a wedding.

# The pre-wedding party...

## Did either of you have a friends-only night out?

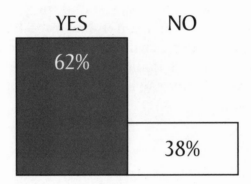

YES         NO

62%

38%

Marlo said: Sure, why not? It's fun to have that one last time out to celebrate your single days and toast to the married times ahead. Exactly how women and men celebrate may vary and often may better be kept quiet.

Barry said: Oh boy! Knowing what I knew about these parties and "having been there and done that," I refused to attend the party of either of my son-in-laws-to-be. My heart would give out.

One of the young grooms wrote us and said his bachelor party was "fantastic." After the bars and several house-to-house parties, they ended up in a house where two strippers came in and the guys went wild. Suddenly, there was a silence when one of the strippers came in and noticed the bride's father and said hello to him by name. Wonder how he knew her?

# Traditional or non-traditional wedding, that is the question?

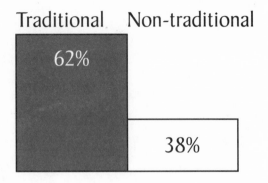

Traditional   Non-traditional

62%

38%

Nontraditional, of course, caught our eye with 38 percent telling us that is what they had. *Here it goes...*

We paid for it all, so we spent as little as possible with the hope of getting large gifts!

Didn't remember more than Las Vegas, getting drunk, woke up the next morning in an Elvis Hotel!

Planned and had the wedding on my due date, and delivered our baby the next morning.

Future husband broke his leg on a ski trip right before the "big day," so we decided to cancel the big affair. Instead, we had a small ceremony at his hospital bedside. The person most upset was my dad, who was paying for the big wedding. He lost a lot of money, but he forgave us anyway.

# Tell us everything about the wedding...

## Number of guests...

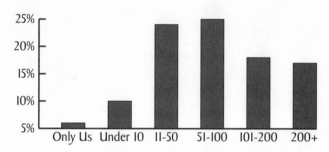

While the average number of guests was 108, one couple reported as many as 600 people at their wedding.

## Cost of the wedding...

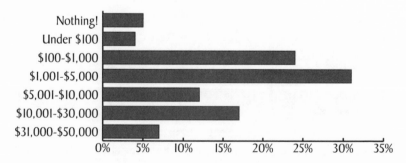

We have couples that spent $75,000, $150,000 and one who spent $250,000 for the 4-6 hours of partying. The average cost of wedding among our newlyweds was $22,311.

Of course every bride needs a wedding dress! Our newlyweds reported paying an average of $1,059 for the once in a lifetime dress. The range was from zero for a hand-me-down to a whopping $25,000 for a custom or designer dress!

Removing the garter continues to be a disappearing part of the wedding ritual, with only 27 percent reporting that they did it at their wedding.

Barry said: I can't bring myself to even talk about the subject of the cost of a wedding, as I made two New York weddings and one Florida wedding with all of them well past the "average." Luckily, all my kids are married and there are no more weddings to pay for!!

Marlo said: I know I can speak for myself, my sister and sister-in-law in saying my mom and dad made us the best weddings a person could ask for! We were all so lucky to have the love and support of such wonderful and generous parents.

# Who paid most of the wedding expenses?

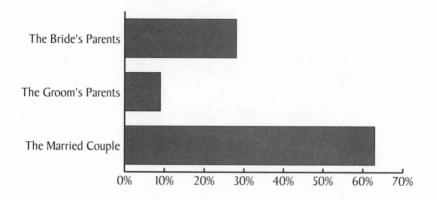

| | |
|---|---|
| The Bride's Parents | |
| The Groom's Parents | |
| The Married Couple | |

0%  10%  20%  30%  40%  50%  60%  70%

Barry said: Why didn't I write this book before making three weddings? I got stuck for them all, while 63 percent of America's couples are footing the bill themselves. Although, one young lady told us that she and her three sisters were all married in the same year, and dear old dad paid for all three weddings. So, at least there is one other poor soul out there.

Marlo said: How lucky are my sister and I? Thanks Dad!

26

# Cheap is cheap, who gave you the cheapest gift?

Is it being cheap or just plain dumb? I guess the cheapskates are those who don't have a clue as to what a wedding costs these days, or perhaps they live in a cave.

The hands down winner is the entire guest list at one wedding. The bride told us: "We had a beautiful expensive wedding with 250 guests, and combined all of the guests gave us a grand total of $849.50". That means the average gift was $3.40 per person, with someone giving even less, resulting in 50 cents! Money isn't everything, but really!

# Were you carried over the threshold?

YES          NO

74%

26%

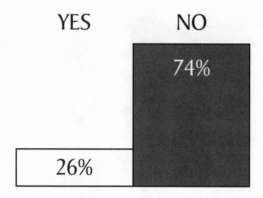

Barry said: A tradition that is slowly expiring. Not only has it dropped to 26 percent, but 56 percent of men couldn't even remember if they did it or not. Those married more than twice are more likely to keep the tradition alive.

# Did anyone try to stop your wedding?

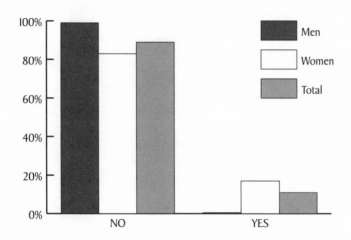

Barry said: According to the men, what this says is that almost no one stood up to stop the wedding. I guess this means that the guys felt that this "particular" guy was indeed the right one for these women.

Marlo said: Watch out guys! This tells us that women are much more in demand. 17 percent of "the crowd," including all boy-friends, girlfriends, relatives, strangers and "others" actually went to some length to try to stop the women from marrying this guy. Why?

# Did your parents raise any doubts about your marriage?

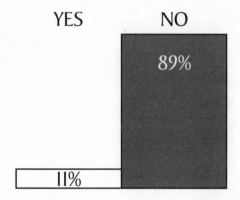

YES          NO

89%

11%

## If they opposed your marriage, why?

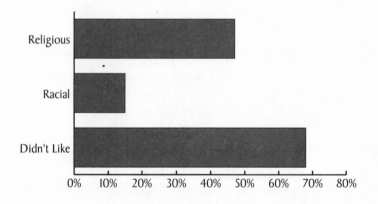

11 percent opposed the marriage with the highest percentage saying, "We just don't like him/her." Religious differences are also high on the list of reasons to oppose the marriage.

# Were any of your old "flames" at the wedding?

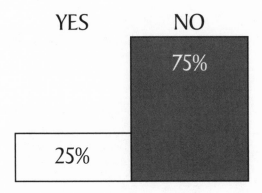

YES       NO

75%

25%

Marlo said: I thought this number would be higher than 25%. So many of my peers have remained friendly with their ex-boyfriends/girlfriends, that I would imagine more would be at the wedding.

Barry said: If I had anything to do with it, I would not allow it. What good could come out of it? Could spell trouble.

# Did you cry at your wedding?

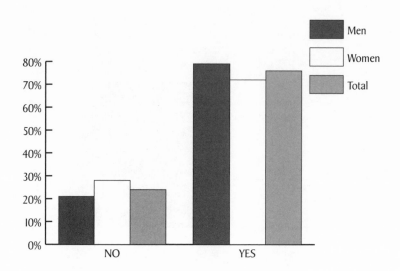

Marlo said: How can you not cry at your own wedding? In fact, I think I cried at every wedding I have ever been to, even those I have watched on television.

Barry said: I cried like a baby at all of the weddings that I made. First, for the sheer joy, second, as a sigh of relief that someone was taking them off my hands and third, because of the money it cost me. Seriously, it is an emotional day for all of the family members involved. ·

# The Honeymoon

## Either of you a virgin?

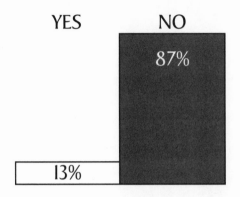

YES                    NO

87%

13%

Barry said: Dust off the sex manuals? 13 percent of our newlyweds told us that at least one of them was a virgin and among that group, 17 percent told us that they were both virgins! Virginity continues to increase as we move into the 21st century after a steady decline from the 60's through the mid 90's.

## If Yes, who?

(Percent among those 13 percent who said yes)

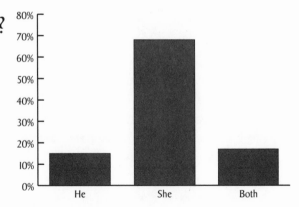

# When you slept together for the first time, did your partner meet your expectations?

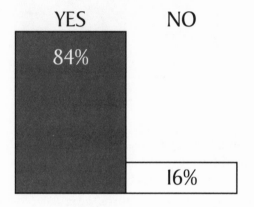

YES          NO

84%

16%

Barry said: Whew! Nearly everyone was satisfied with their partner. Just 16 percent were not satisfied. And guess what? 80 percent of those not satisfied were the women, who said they had to teach their man the right way to do it. Just about everyone now reports that through communication everyone has gotten an A+.

# Did you make love on your wedding night?

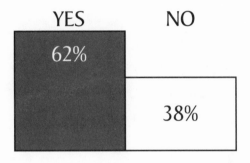

YES 62%

NO 38%

Barry said: "Why is this night different than all others," an old proverb? It appears NOT! 38 percent of our newlyweds did NOT make love on this the wedding night. Impossible, unheard of, why get married… those are all adjectives from the past. With so many people living together, it appears that this night is just like all the rest. They told us they were too tired, didn't even think about it, stayed up all night with their friends, too exhausted, busy counting money and looking at gifts, or had to catch a plane for their honeymoon. What a difference 40 years makes!

# On average, how often did you make love on your honeymoon?

## Times Per Day...

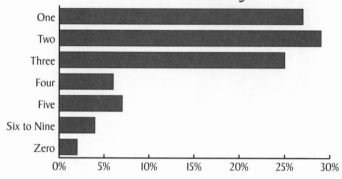

(Ten or more time per day:  3 couples!)

Marlo said:  No comment!

Barry said:  I am tired just looking at this chart. These people made love 2.74 times a day, with 3 couples telling us they did it 14, 16 and 18 times a day.  How can their marriage last after the honeymoon when they won't have any time to go to work?  I am intrigued by the 2 percent who told us that they didn't make love at all on their honeymoon, just what were they doing?  Maybe they were watching the 3 couples who were doing it more than 10 times a day, and they themselves were worn out.

# Chapter 3

Honeymoon is over
and real life begins.

# Do you have sex more since you have been married?

Barry said: All I want to say is: Can you imagine asking this question 30 years ago!

Marlo said: Doesn't surprise me. So many couples have been together for quite a while before getting married that the honeymoon began long before the walk down the aisle. I am, however, a bit surprised at how high the number is with 72 percent saying they had more sex before being "officially" married. Why the sudden change? After all, it is a lot easier when you live together in your own home with your own privacy day in and day out.

# Do you find lovemaking is better now that you are married?

YES       NO

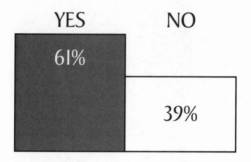

61%

39%

Marlo said: Quantity, Quality, Quantity, Quality!

While 72 percent of our newlyweds said they had more sex BEFORE they were married, 61 percent tell us their lovemaking is better. So the survey says, the quality has improved while the quantity has been reduced. So here's to quality time!

# What one thing did you let your spouse see, do, or know only after you were married?

Barry said:  No comment!

Marlo said:  Read among yourselves, laugh and relate.

| | |
|---|---|
| He bathes me | That I have bad gas |
| My temper | Spots on my arms |
| Pictures of when I was fat | Dentures |
| Masturbating | Farting |
| My laziness | Walking around naked |
| My naked body in full light | My sexual fantasy |
| More of my feelings | In the bathroom with me |
| Changing Tampons | Me without makeup |

Best Answer: " I introduced her to my imaginary friend."

# What are the best and worst qualities of your spouse?

Barry and Marlo say: These are genuinely very funny and very, very strange. Enjoy.

| BEST | WORST |
|------|-------|
| His butt | His butt |
| Her butt | Her butt |
| His penis | His small penis |
| Easy to talk to | Never stops talking |
| Very understanding | Irresponsible |
| Good personality | Smelly feet |
| Sense of humor | Possessive |
| Good in bed | No foreplay |
| Very good in bed | Not enough foreplay |
| Great in bed | Too neat |
| Sexy | Too messy |
| Unselfish | Leaves toilet seat up |
| Always ready for sex | Total slob |
| Very loving | Never stops eating |
| Honest | Exaggerates |
| Faithful | Always interrupting me |
| Nice looking | Too much sports |
| Patient | Procrastinator |
| Her breasts | Her breasts |
| Compassionate | No compassion |
| Intelligent | Stupid |
| Pampers me | Sex only when she wants it |
| Affectionate | Can't read lips |

Ok, folks, now sit down and write down which qualities match those of your mate!

# Pampered? What are the most unusual ways that your spouse does this?

Barry said: I wish I could get my wife to do some of these things.

Marlo said: I gave my husband my own list and told him to start thinking.

Is your mate as wonderful as these kind, understanding, considerate, go out of their way newlyweds? Just look at what these people do for each other.

Scratch his back
Rub her feet
Talk baby talk
Treat her like a tramp
Give him a bubble bath
Buy him a 12-pack
Watch sports with him
Cut his nails
Give in
Put out
Sex whenever he wants
Suck her toes
Wash him after sex
Oral sex even though I hate it

Shave his neck hair
Make Pop Tarts
Bake brownies for her
He lets me beat him
Take a bath with her
Drink with him
Clean up for her
Polish her nails
Give up
Sex whenever she wants
Give her a sponge bath
Clean his ears
Lick her all over
Lets me have my way

Best Answer: "He does me a great favor by staying up more than five minutes after we make love, and sometimes he even talks to me."

43

# How often do you say the magic words, "I love you?"

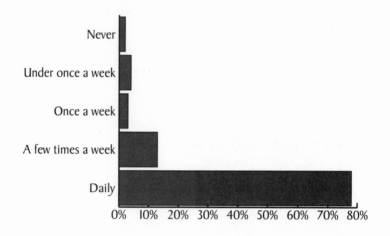

| | |
|---|---|
| Never | |
| Under once a week | |
| Once a week | |
| A few times a week | |
| Daily | |

0%  10%  20%  30%  40%  50%  60%  70%  80%

Barry said: You can't disagree with me on this one. After nearly 40 years of marriage we never go a single day without saying "I love you." To see that 22 percent of these newly-weds don't do that is just unbelievable to me. It takes less than a second to say it and why in the world wouldn't you? The 2 percent who never say it are obviously married to the wrong person.

Marlo said: Dad is right on with this one. I learned this from him and my mom. I never let a day go by without saying "I love you" to my husband and he does the same.

44

# Are the two of you ever in the bathroom at the same time?

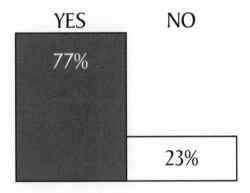

Barry said: My wife will share the bathroom with  anyone, anywhere, any time. We found that the older newlyweds, those over 40 are less apt to share the bathroom with their spouse. The high income group (75k+) are also very much bathroom shy. Does this mean anything to any of you?

Marlo said: Sharing the bathroom for brushing teeth, blow-drying hair and bubble baths are okay. I draw the line there. Personal hygeine and bowel habits demand privacy!!

# Do you leave the bathroom toilet seat up more often than not?

YES        NO

81%

19%

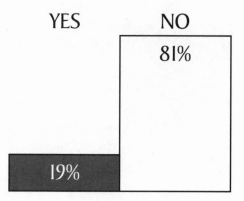

Barry said: I knew we were not that bad, but it is interesting that more men (32 percent) admitted to this alleged dreadful deed than the women who (27 percent) said it is a habit that drives them crazy. That would mean that 5 percent of the men or women are not even aware of it. A tidbit: a higher percentage of the lower income families are more likely to be the leaver-uppers than those in the higher income brackets.

Marlo said: I want a recount, these figures can't possibly be correct. I never met a toilet seat that is in the right position in my house.

# Talk, Talk, Talk.
# Do you set aside time in your
# day to talk together?

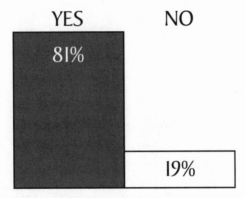

YES         NO

81%

19%

Barry said: I am pleasantly surprised that 81 percent of our newlyweds communicate. I have always said that communication is perhaps the most important part of a successful marriage. A word to the unwise 19 percent, get your act together and find time to sit and talk every single day. Your future is at stake.

Marlo said: As busy as my husband and I are, both working 8-10 hours a day and taking care of 3 children, we always find a few minutes to just sit down and talk. It is so very important. Think about it, with the invention of cellular phones, you can talk to each other anywhere, anytime!

# How many times a day is enough for you, talking to your spouse on the phone that is!

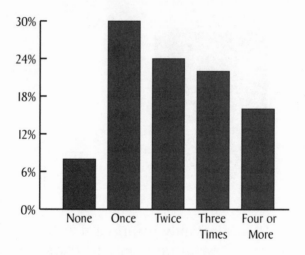

Barry said: Money is flowing to the phone companies as our newlyweds speak to one another an average of 3.3 times a day. They can't get enough of each other at home so they must report in on everything that happens when they are apart.

Marlo said: We have some couples who told us that they call each other 10, 15, 20 times a day. Those are mostly the couples where both are working. I guess they don't have enough to do at work so why not chat with each other. In our family, the cell phone bills skyrocket because we speak to each other just about every hour, or so it seems.

# Who is more romantic?

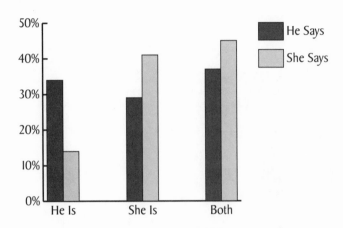

Marlo said: This is a "he said, she said" question, but the women prevail by a wide margin when you add it all up. Women are definitely more romantic, no matter what he says.

Barry said: My only defense is that the youngest group of newlyweds, under 24, tell us that the men are more romantic than the women. All other groups tell us it is the female side of the ledger that is more romantic.

# When you leave for work do you kiss good bye?

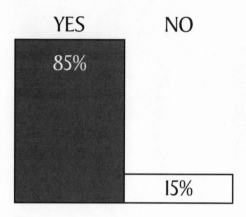

YES        NO

85%

15%

Barry said: It's not the 85 percent of our newlyweds, including the rich, the not so rich, the old and young who plant a kiss on their beloved before they leave for the day that is surprising. It is the 15 percent who say they don't that leaves me baffled. What are these newlyweds thinking? They just got married, are newly in love and they don't kiss goodbye everyday, what is that about?

Marlo said: Neither of us would ever leave the house without a kiss goodbye. It is as routine as brushing your teeth, how can you not want to do that?

# Look out! Do you have an adoring, or not so adoring, nickname for your spouse?

## What you told us...

| | | | |
|---|---|---|---|
| Babe | Crazy | Moron | Sillyhead |
| Baby | Dopeyhead | Mr. Smith | Smokey |
| Baby Cakes | Frisky | Muff | Snuggle Muffin |
| Baby Doll | Fuzzy Butt | Muffy | Squishy Fuzzy |
| Babykins | Handsome Man | My Chick | Sugar Woogum |
| Beermeister | Honey | My Guy | Sweetheart |
| Big Bear | Honeybunch | My Life, My Love | Sweetie |
| Big Kahuna | Honey Bunny | Pokey | Sweetmeat |
| Blondie | Honeypie | Pooh Bear | Sweet Pea |
| Boy | Hooter | Pook | Taffy |
| Bubba | Horney Honey | Poopie | Turkey |
| Buddah | Johnson | Pretty Lady | Wiggle Butt |
| Coach | Kat | Pumpkin | Will |
| Cowboy | Kid | Pussycat | Woman |
| Cupcake | Kitten | Putz | |
| Cutie | Liver Lips | Redman | |
| Cutie Pie | Lovey | Silly | |

Barry said: Is there any one of us who hasn't endeared our spouse with some loving or not so loving words when getting their attention? Beware, some of these are definitely not "G" rated! Some of these defy description!

# What are the reasons you married your spouse?

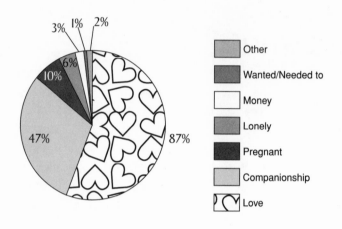

**Legend:**
- Other
- Wanted/Needed to
- Money
- Lonely
- Pregnant
- Companionship
- Love

Marlo said: Ecch! Lonely, money, pregnant, companion-ship… what happened to everyone marrying for love?

Barry Said: In a rare moment, I agree with Marlo. I find it totally crazy that only 87% married for love. Can that really be? 47% said they also married for companionship. These people must be kidding! If it isn't 100% love, then you shouldn't get married.

# Do you wear your wedding ring?

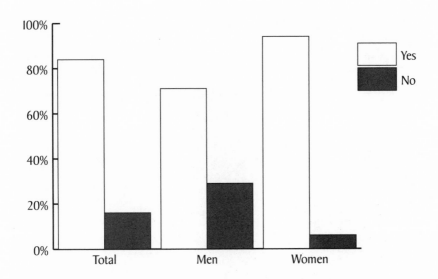

Marlo said: My husband tried the "I never wear jewelry" and "What if my fingers swell" trick before we were married. Now, he wouldn't even think of taking his ring off.

Barry said: So, 29 percent of the men must have some kind of allergic reaction to wearing gold. It is understandable, except in my house, where mine is hermetically sealed on my finger and can never be taken off! Those that don't wear the ring are in the upper income bracket and generally over 40 years old.

# Spend more time with your friends or your spouse's friends?

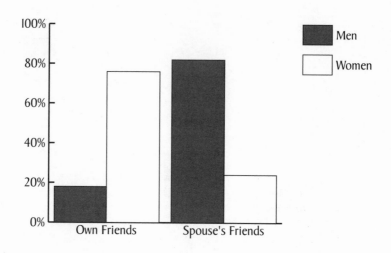

Marlo said: It seems to be a fact that when a guy ties the knot he not only takes a bride, but his bride's best friends as well. That girl to girl bond is hard to break! We welcome all the husbands to our circles!

 Barry said: The only group that is the exception to this unwritten rule are the under 24 guys. These men seem to have kept it their way when it comes to friends. Hang in there ladies, it won't be long before you take over!

# Has your spouse taken a vacation without you since the wedding?

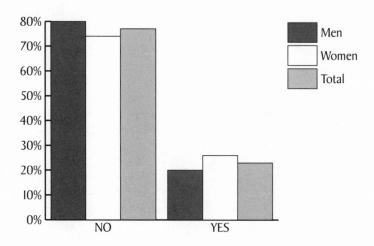

Barry said: It remains a man's world in at least this one instance. Only married a short time and already more men, 26 percent versus 20 percent of women, have vacationed without their spouse. After 38+ years of marriage I look forward to the times that my wife goes to visit the children and grandchildren without me. That is my only vacation alone!

Marlo said: It is out of the question in my family. My husband would never even think of it, and for that matter I wouldn't either.

# How often do you speak to your parents since you are married?

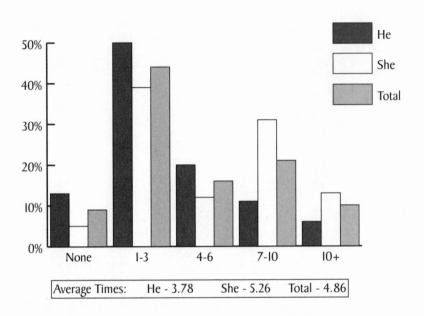

Average Times:   He - 3.78   She - 5.26   Total - 4.86

Barry said:  This is where all the trouble starts at the beginning of a marriage and continues until who knows when. Nearly half of the wives talk to their parents more than 10 times a week! While us guys speak to our parents less than 4 times a week.  Quite a difference.

Marlo said: Who else are we going to talk to if not mom and dad?  In fact, I am surprised that the average is only 5.26 times a week.  I speak to my parents at least 3 times a day, but don't tell my husband…..they are all long distance calls.

# How often do you speak to your wonderful in-laws?

Barry said:  Virtually all of us who gave a "truthful" answer said "as little as possible."  Is it any wonder that it is mostly men who gave that answer?

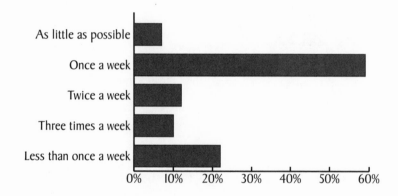

Marlo said:  On the other end of the spectrum, truth be let it known that us wonderful "daughter-in-laws" speak to our in-laws three times a week usually because our husbands are too busy or too lazy!

# What do you call your in-laws?

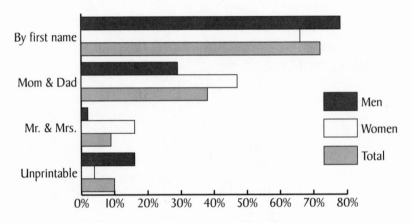

By first name
Mom & Dad
Mr. & Mrs.
Unprintable

Men
Women
Total

0%  10%  20%  30%  40%  50%  60%  70%  80%

* adds to more than 100 percent due to multiple answers

Barry said: As an "old timer," I thought the answers to this question were very different than what I would have thought they would be. In my day, it was "mom and dad"; no ifs, ands or buts! Four times as many men as women, however, fall into the "unprintable" category, as is illustrated above.

Marlo said: I thought these answers are right in line with what all of my friends do and that is first names are usually the way to go. Some of those married for a longer period of time have taken to mom and dad. I do agree that the men are just not nice when it comes to the unprintable stuff!

# Sex life routine, since you got married?

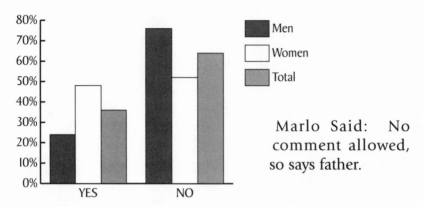

Marlo Said: No comment allowed, so says father.

Barry said: What gives? Doesn't it take two to make it happen the fun way? More than one-third say their sex life has become routine. This is terrible for newlyweds, but more startling is that only 24 percent of men seem to think it is routine while nearly half of the women feel that way. It sure seems time for a talk among the couples about what is going on between the sheets.

However, if you don't want your sex life to become routine, our newlyweds send along these suggestions: (Try at your own risk!)

| | |
|---|---|
| Tying each other up | Toys |
| Sex in the car | Sex in the office |
| Sex at her mother's home | New positions |
| Have him wait a week | Role-playing |

# Fantasies...do you?
# About your spouse, others,
# and do you tell?

## Fantasize about your spouse?

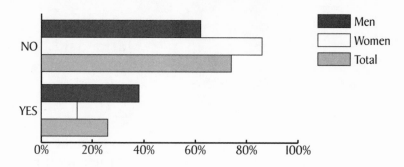

## If yes, do you tell your spouse about the fantasies?

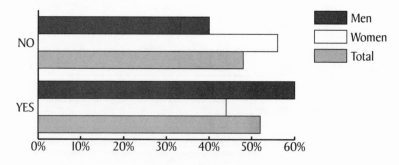

** Percentages based ONLY on those who answered YES.

# Do you tell your spouse about the people in your fantasies?

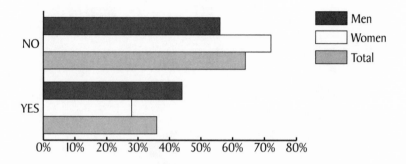

** Percentages based ONLY on those who answered YES.

Barry said: Are you surprised that it is the newly-wed men who have fantasy on their minds? They have more fantasies overall, they tell more and don't stop there...they even tell about the people in their fantaises! Are their wives actually listening?

Marlo said: I hope the women are good listeners! These men have a lot to say and they had better be good. The most likely fantasizers are in the 25-34 year old age group and tend to be those that earn less than $30k a year.

# Who initiates lovemaking more often?

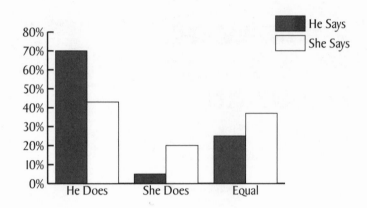

Barry says: Old vs. new thinking. It used to be a man's world, but that is changing, although women still have a way to go. You would expect that they can't agree, as 70% of the men say it is "He" who initiates lovemaking, versus 43% of women who say it is "She."

Marlo says: As an old romantic who still believes in chivalry, I am glad to see men are still initiating in most cases. But, hey, sometimes it takes a women to get things going, so that is okay, too.

# BEFORE AND AFTER

How many times a day did you and do you have a loving thought about your spouse? First tell us about before you were married and secondly, since you are married?

## BEFORE

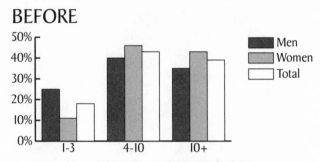

Averages: Men=8.55, Women=9.89, Total= 9.22

## AFTER

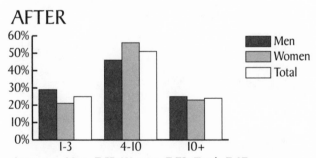

Averages: Men=7.55, Women=7.79, Total=7.67

Our couples have cooled it a bit since donning the gold rings. They both have less loving thoughts a day after getting married. Women's thoughts dropped by twice as much as did the men's. Maybe the women are working harder and have less time to think about their man.

63

# How did you really, really feel about the size of your engagement ring?

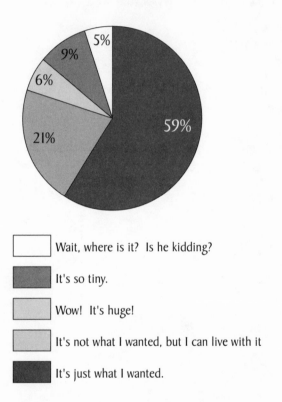

Wait, where is it?  Is he kidding?

It's so tiny.

Wow!  It's huge!

It's not what I wanted, but I can live with it

It's just what I wanted.

35 percent of the women had a little problem with the ring. They obviously wanted more, more, more.  Only 6 percent of the women were astounded, delighted and thrilled at the size of the ring.  It appears 5 percent were more than disappointed with the size.

# Do you shower together?

88 percent of our newly-weds shower together from time to time, with 20 percent doing it regularly, that is more than twice a week.

58 percent have made love in the shower and 16 percent say they do it several times a week.
They are also late to work on those days!

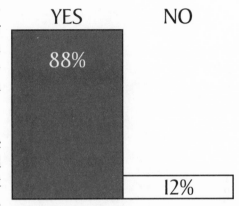

# Do you ever make love in the shower?

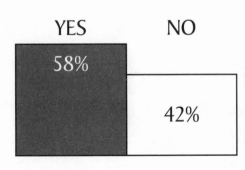

Of the 12 percent who have not made love in the shower, nearly all have said they are getting ready to try it. What a great energy saver, showering together and making love at the same time!

# Do you usually watch the same programs on tv together?

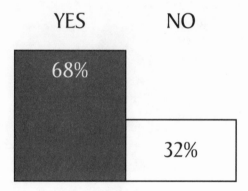

YES       NO

68%

32%

Sixty-eight percent of our newlyweds love to spend time watching the same television programs, while the remaining thirty two percent represent a combination of fighting for control or moving to another room.

# Who controls the remote? (like we don't know!)

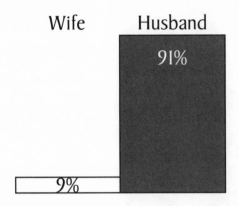

Wife      Husband

91%

9%

Barry said: What is becoming of my fellowman, would you believe only 91 percent of husbands hold onto the remote control? How can it be that a full 9 percent of wives have wrestled control of this most sacred ritual that is rightfully a man's possession? I am genuinely frightened at this trend. I did everything I could to track down the women who have taken control of our rightful possession and they have the following profile:

She most likely lives in Connecticut, Missouri, California and Florida. She is probably slightly over 35 years old. She is in big-time-earning home, over $75,000. And she may have been married more than once. Please be on the look out for these woman and stop this trend.

Marlo said: Hey ladies, let him think he is in control. If the remote makes him happy, you have nothing to worry about!

# In what position do you actually sleep?

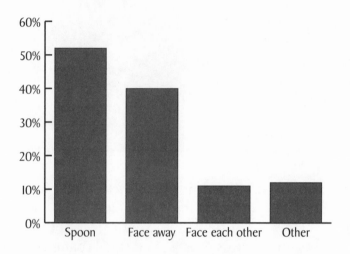

*Adds to more than 100 percent due to multiple answers

Spooning is the favored position by far, but more interesting is the 12 percent who said they sleep in the "other position." Wouldn't you like to know what that is? One on the floor and one on the bed, on top of each other, one room for each, who knows?

# Are you more sexy now that you are married?

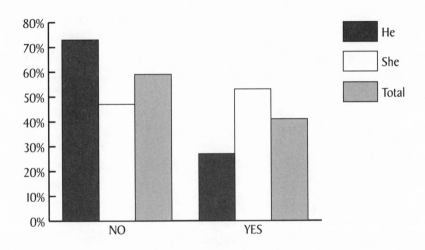

Barry said: This question makes me wish I were 35 years younger because 41 percent of our couples have told us that they have become sexier. In this instance, it means that they have experienced new and exciting things to spice up their sex lives. When we look at the overall data we do have a statistical quirk or a bunch of liars, fakers or exaggerators. While 27 percent of men have become sexier, nearly twice as many women (53 percent) say they have become sexier. It makes you wonder what is going on and is it a joint or separate effort if you know what I mean.

# What new things are you doing sexually?

Now for the skinny on what exactly is going on specifically. The following is a partial list of what new things our couples are doing sexually that they didn't experience before. Again, we caution, do not try these things alone, I think?

| | |
|---|---|
| Teach him/her to perform oral sex | Make love outdoors |
| Find that special spot | Experiment more with fruit |
| Make love in public places | Watch x-rated movies |
| Tie each other up | Have her wear my underwear |
| Have him wear my panties | Use vibrators |
| Masturbate each other | Talk dirty |
| Use sex toys | Become the aggressor |

Best answer:
"Don't think of my mother watching me do this."

Who are they? Among women, it is the under 24 year old group that are the top experimentors. Among men, it is the 25-34 year old group.

# Sex, sex and more sex

Barry said: I used my statistical skills to create the great American sex life in a new marriage table below. Basically, we asked about the number of times that these newlyweds made love during the first year of the marriage. So I added, divided, multiplied, by days, weeks, months, hours and such and came up with something that is quite revealing and it looks like this:

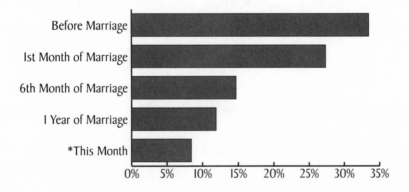

\* The last thirty days regardless of how long they have been married.

Our newlyweds practically gave me a heart attack! Remember, I have been married for nearly 40 years, and I find it hard to believe and very wishful thinking. I even refused to let Marlo look at this table and certainly I don't want to hear her answers.

Before marriage, our couples were making love more than once a day on average! Can you possibly imagine that? When did they have time to watch tv, eat and go to work? My, what energy they must have had!

As soon as the bell rung, the wedding bell that is, they slowed down to only a bit less than once a day during the first month of marriage, by month six it was down to once every two days and at the end of a year it was even less. During the past 30 days regardless of how long they were married (and some have been married for as long as two years) the number was even less, at just a tad over once a week. Are our newlyweds running out of stamina already? I find these to be incredible numbers while very interesting at the same time.

# Do you undress in front of your mate?

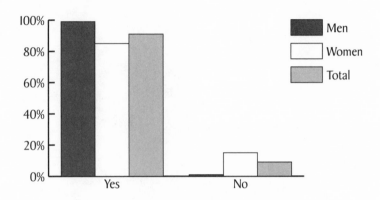

Barry said: In the "olden" days many husbands and wives never ever saw each other in their "birthday suits." In speaking to the older generation, those who are now in their 70's, 80's, 90's, tell us that they themselves still never undress in front of their mate.

 Marlo said: You are married, you are making love, why hold back now? I can't imagine it is time to be shy now! Still, 15 percent remain too shy to wear their birthday suits in front of thier partner. However, as my dad said, nearly all of them were in the 65+ age group. There was a few "shy" women under 24 who told us the same, though.

# Have you ever asked your partner to change lovemaking techniques? What happened??

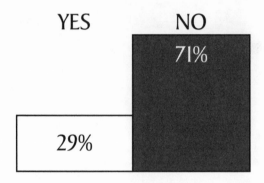

YES            NO

71%

29%

Barry said: Talk about a "touchy feely" sensitive question, no pun intended. Lovemaking in the 21st century has taken us to new heights. 29 percent of our newlyweds (how experienced can any of them be) have actually asked their partner to change some part of their technique while making love.

The "change," however, brought a whole different set of rules. When women asked the man to change his technique, he obliged in 96 percent of the cases. But when the man asked his wife to change, only 60 percent went along with it.

Seems like our male newlyweds could use a course in persuasive speaking or the females should listen better! (No cards and letters please)

# Do you think your spouse has ever been unfaithful to you?

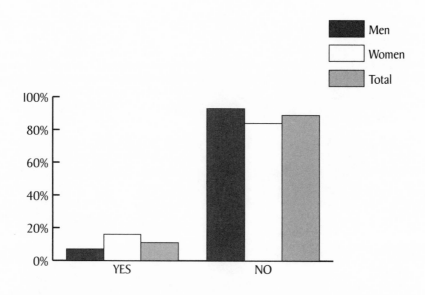

Barry said: There is trouble brewing on the ladies side of the bed as more than twice as many women, 16 percent versus 7 percent for men, think that their spouse has been unfaithful.

Marlo said: I believe that the total of 11 percent who think their spouse has been unfaithful is an extremely high number for newlyweds.

# Have you ever made love to a sleeping partner?

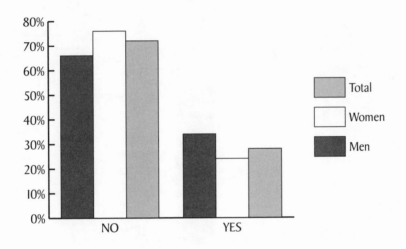

Barry said: This is one of the more bizarre questions in our book. Has anyone ever thought of, much less been asked this question. Well, 28 percent of our extremely frisky newlyweds have told us that yes, they have made love to their partner while their partner was sleeping!

34 percent of men (bizarre, but possible) and 24 percent of women have done this deed. I wouldn't dare think too much about this one!

# Did you finish or did your partner awaken?

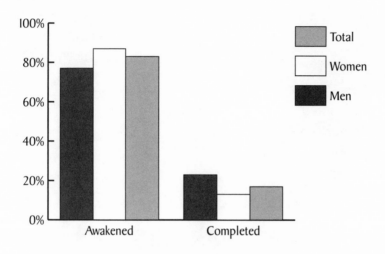

Barry said: "And in conclusion".... I need some sex thera-
pists to help me with this one because it is way beyond me.
28 percent of our newlyweds admit to trying to make love to
their partner while they are asleep and so it brings
to question that 23 percent of these men said they com-
pleted the act, while 13 percent of the women said they com-
pleted the act. Needless to say, I can understand how men
can claim to have done this, but I find it hard to
understand how the women can do this successfully. I just
hope that everyone is having fun doing this.

# Do you go to the bathroom before making love?

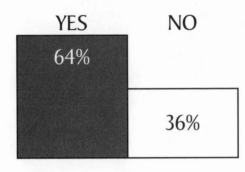

YES 64%    NO 36%

Barry said:
Can you spell spontaneity! It seems to have gone out the window for more than a third of our newlyweds.

# Do you go to the bathroom after making love?

Newlyweds are running and flushing from coast to coast! It looks like there is a stampede to the bathroom immediately following making love. Is that you?

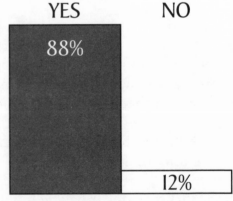

YES 88%    NO 12%

# What is your favorite sexual position?

Barry said: This is a question that at my age I don't have to know about. It is too much information for me and I certainly will not allow my daughter to comment on this subject, as I am the father and that's why! But, in the public interest the following are the answers provided to us in no particular order:

(Try them at your own risk)

| | |
|---|---|
| In a public place… standing up! | Tied up |
| At work, on the copier | Hips on pillow |
| Back to back | Sixty-nine |
| Any way | Sixty-three? |
| Every way | With legs on his shoulders |
| With my wife on top | Upside down |
| With my husband on bottom | Doggie style |
| Sitting down on top of me | With my mother-in-law sleeping in the next room, and my wife holding my mouth |
| In the boss's office on his desk when he goes home | |
| Number 26 in the sex book my mother bought for me | |

Note to newlyweds: I sure hope you carry accident insurance!

# What is your favorite place at home to make love other than the bedroom?

Marlo said: Dad let me take this one. Here are the answers, again in no particular order. Love comes in all shapes and sizes and amazing places:

| | |
|---|---|
| Living room couch | Living room table |
| Bathroom floor | Living room floor |
| Hallway stairs | Bathroom on the toilet |
| Pool table | Garage |
| Garage in the car | Garage on the car |
| Den | Basement |
| Weight Bench | Backyard |
| Pool Deck | Shower |
| Kitchen | In front of fireplace |
| Kids' beds | |

# Have you ever made love
# in your car?

Barry said: Oh! Those ladies. 60 percent of all of our new-lywed brides have told us that they have indeed made love in a car as compared to only 46 percent of the men. The women who admit to this are generally under 24 and they have done it on an average of 4 times.

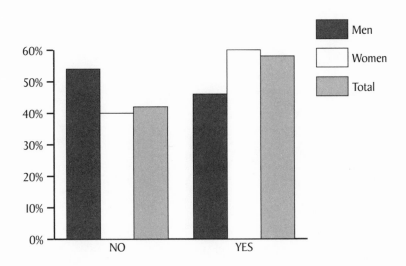

# Have you ever made love in the car while driving?

Barry said: And people are furious about talking on the cell phone while driving? How about the 15 percent of our newlyweds who say they have made love in a moving car! 22 percent of men and 8 percent of the women have done this, wonder if they were on the phone at the time!

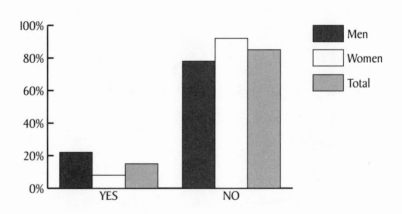

Marlo said: Do you think they were wearing seat belts?

# What do you fight about most often?

Marlo said: This list is so long it would take up an entire book. So, we have limited it to the best of the best. See if your hot topics are among this list.

Jealousy

Leisure time

Trust

Lying

Having children

Bossiness

In-laws

# What is the most annoying thing your mother in-law does?

The question for the ages. Mother-in-law jokes are as old as time. Most mother-in-laws do not deserve the the criticism thrown at them although some fully deserve it. The following are some of the wonderful things that mother-in-laws do to cause stress on a marriage...........enjoy!

| |
|---|
| Gives my kids things they are not supposed to have |
| Gives us money, then holds it over our heads |
| Offers her opinion on everything |
| Always makes my wife feel bad |
| Upsets my husband |
| Takes his side all the time |
| Takes her side all the time |
| Sits around while everyone else works |
| Complains, complains, complains |
| Smokes like a chimney |
| Won't talk to me |
| Won't acknowledge me |

| |
|---|
| Hates me |
| Is very judgemental |
| Is always negative |
| Complains about ex-President Clinton |
| Talks about how wonderful President Bush is |
| Pleads poverty then goes out and buys a new Mercedes |
| Makes my husband do the dishes |
| Believe's she's beautiful |
| Is a witch |
| Is a bitch |
| Calls too much |
| Watches soap operas 24 hours a day |
| Lives with us |
| Cheats at cards |
| Only hears what she wants |
| Babies her son |
| Compares my husband to her other sons |

# Have any of your spouse's friends come on to you?

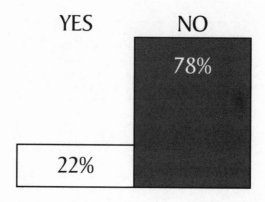

YES        NO

78%

22%

# If yes, did you tell?

Of the 22 percent who said yes....Did you tell?

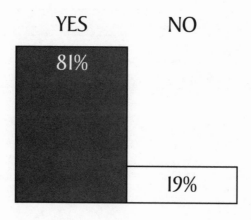

YES        NO

81%

19%

Marlo said: This one is a total surprise for a number of reasons. Most of these people are married less than a year, and 22 percent already have "friends" coming on to their spouses. What kind of friends are these, anyway?

Now for the surprising things: It was more of the "female friends" that have come on to the newlywed husbands than the reverse. I would have thought that the women would be the most likely of the two to get "hit on".

And what happens afterward? Another amazing surprise or not? 91 percent of the men told their wives about being hit on, while only 28 percent of the women took time to tell their husbands.

# JEALOUS?
# Are you jealous of your spouse's opposite sex friends?

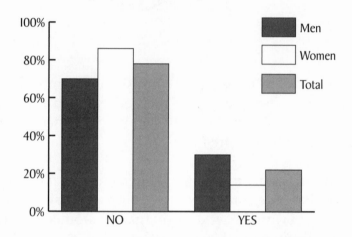

Marlo said: By a wide margin, our husbands are so jealous of our "guy" friends. It is both silly and great at the same time. It keeps them on their toes, but is really harmless. After all, neither of you can expect to have friends of only your sex.

And would you believe 81 percent of these most possessive husbands even put limitations on their wives' friendships with these guys? Limitations include: no visiting when he's not home (whether he has gone to the store, is at work or out of town), and no calling or seeing without him being present. Many husbands declare that he sees all correspondence and that there is absolutely no so-called "friendly" kissing. Insecure or what?

# Have you developed an attraction to any of your spouse's friends?

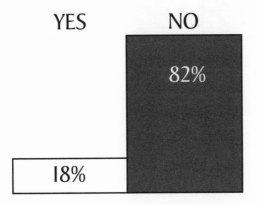

YES      NO

82%

18%

Marlo said: I cannot believe it is even that high, but 18 percent can be harmless, as long as it is only an attraction, and it is not acted upon! Most of these people are men and women in the 25-34 year old age group. I would keep my eyes wide, wide open!

# Propositioned?

## By you?

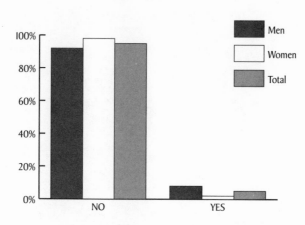

## To you?

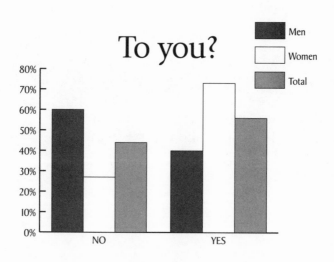

Marlo said: This is the real deal, not just do you have an attraction for someone, this is the real thing, if you know what I mean! Only a very small percentage (5 percent) of our newlyweds have done the propositioning. By 4 to 1, it is the men. Not a nice proportion for this proposition.

Recipients of a proposition, while in the eyes of the beholder is quite rampant as the majority (56 percent) have reported being given more than the eye. 40 percent of men and nearly three quarters (73 percent) of the women have reported these unwanted propositions. At least that is what over 90 percent told us.

Interestingly enough, the people most likely to do the propositioning or receive the proposition, are the same people, in the "under 24" category; married for the first time, with lots of money. Quite a proposition, don't you think?

# Would you mind if your spouse went to a strip bar?

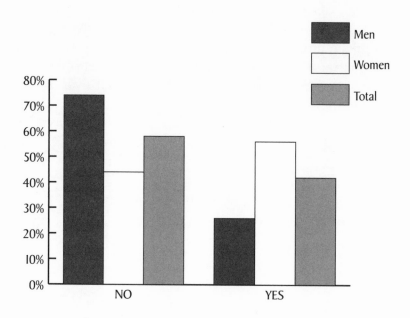

Barry said: To strip or not to strip with strangers, that is the question. Newlywed women are right on as only 26 percent said they would NOT like it if their man went to a strip club. This doesn't hold true for the men who said a resounding NO to 56 percent of the women! So, it is good for the goose but not the gander! Those women who give their blessings are more than likely to be in the older group (40+ years old), probably because the men at that age can't see or hear very well and are harmless.

# Do you ever take your wedding ring off when you leave the house?

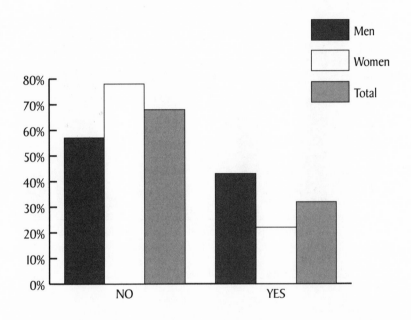

Men
Women
Total

Marlo said: Strange things are happening in about one third of our newlywed households. 32 percent actually told us that they sometimes remove their wedding ring when they leave the house. No surprise to me that twice as many men (43 percent) as women (22 percent) are likely to do this. As long as they are heading to the gym and not to the bars or clubs, I suppose it is okay.

# What do you wear to sleep?

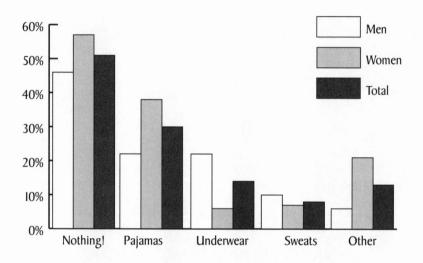

Note: * Adds up to more than 100 percent due to multiple answers.

Marlo said:  I suppose pajamas sales are down!  If you catch our newlyweds sleep walking, you will find half of them in the nude.  More women (57 percent) than men (46 percent), but nonetheless the trend is on bare skin!

# Do you usually go to bed at the same time?

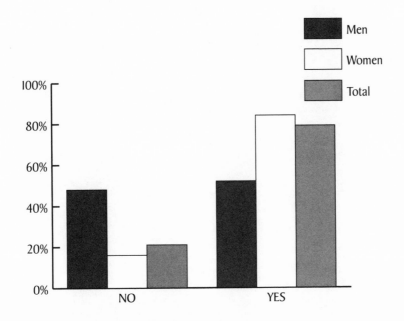

Barry said: This appears to be a case of possible hanky-panky, the missing husband, or the wife who sleeps so deeply that she doesn't know he is missing. 84 percent of women and 52 percent of men say that they go to bed at "the same time." What's wrong with that picture? My hypothesis is that there are a whole bunch of sleeping wives when the husbands catch a second wind and leave the marital bed. Can their be another explanation in this descrepancy?

# Chapter 4

Real stories: some sad, some funny, all poignant and the statistics about who these newlyweds are and aren't

# This is who the newlyweds in our book are:

They have been married an average of 10.45 months when they filled out our questionnaires.

74 percent are married for the first time.

72 percent had no children at the time, but 16 percent are pregnant.

Those who do have children from previous marriages have an average of 2.1 children from his marriage and 1.7 from her marriage.

Our newlyweds are on average 32 years old, with an age range of 18 to 91.

The average household income is $52,345; 83 percent are two-income families.

32 percent earn less than $30,000 a year, and 21 percent earn more than $75,000 a year.

64 percent attended or graduated from college.

36 percent are urbanites, 16 percent live in rural areas, 48 percent are suburbanites.

53 percent live in a single-family home, 43 percent live in an apartment.

45 percent of the respondents are male while 55 percent are female.

# Newlywed stories!

At the end of our questionnaire, we asked our newlyweds to tell us anything that they wanted about their relationships with their spouse, starting with the time they met up until the present day. We received more than 2,400 wonderful stories, but due to space limitations we had to choose only a few. They will make you laugh, they will make you cry. Enjoy!

One day, at just before 5 pm, my boss called and asked me to come to his office. I was very nervous, as I had never been called to his office before and only worked there a short time. The other people in my office thought I was going to get fired, and I was quite afraid. When I got to his office, he told me that he had been watching me and that he was in love with me even though we had never met. It didn't take long before he seduced me and we made love in his office that night. Then he took me out to dinner and from that day on we were inseparable, he asked me to marry him and I did. Needless to say, the people in my office were quite surprised, not as surprised as I was. They all seemed to "know what happened," it probably was because of the very big smile on my face the next morning when I came to work.

After we got married, we stayed at home for our honeymoon, and I became very sick. At first, I thought I had food poisoning. I was vomiting like crazy. My husband ended up taking me to the emergency room. Within a few minutes, the vomiting stopped and they told me I did not have food poisoning. It turned out I was four months pregnant. It was the best wedding present that we got.

I don't have a lot to brag about. I've been very disappointed with this marriage. It's my fourth, and I have to stick it out because everyone said it wouldn't last. They were right, but I can't let them know. I can't stand this man. He is 78 years old but looks 95. I am 73 and look 50. He's a short-tempered, self-centered and, generally, a pain in the ass. He was a preacher, but he is meaner than a junkyard dog. You see, he is jealous and resentful that I am more educated than he is, so he embarrasses me all the time. I can't tell if he is crazy, or what. I just hope I outlive him as I've done with husbands one and three.

The most exciting part of our relationship is that we had been 'just friends' for about two years. One night we went to the movies together, and I bought popcorn and a soda for her. As I leaned over to give them to her, our lips brushed, and she kissed me. It was so intense and overwhelming and I think we both wanted it, but dared to say it because we had been friends for so long. Needless to say, our friendship ended that night and we fell madly in love. I love her so very much and we were married three months ago, after being friends for three years.

The bakery that made my wedding cake was held up on my wedding day by a crazed man who wanted to kill himself, and the owners of the store for an unkown reason. He held them hostage for five hours until, believe it or not, he fell asleep. The baker escaped, called the police and then, would you believe, he personally brought the cake three hours late, but about one hour before we were to toast and cut it. We asked him to stay for the rest of the reception. It was quite a story; it even made the local news that night!

I have three children, ages 17, 14 and 10 and my second husband has four children, ages 16, 14, 12 and 10. We got married two months ago, and all the children participated in the wedding party. It was a wonderful day, sort of like the Brady Bunch wedding. Well, I took sick about a month after the wedding and my husband took me to the doctor. I was a bit frightened because I thought I had something very serious. The doctor examined me and told us to wait in his office. In the few minutes we had to wait, my entire life flashed in front of me, and both my husband and I were extremely quiet in anticipation of some terrible news. The doctor soon came back and calmly told us that I was pregnant at age 45. My husband fainted as he sat next to me, and I took a deep breath, thankful that I wasn't dying.

I immediately began to cry and laugh at the same time. When we got home, we had to wait seven hours until all seven children were at home. We sat them down in the living room and told them that they were going to have a new sibling. At first, they didn't understand, then they went berserk with joy! They kidded us to no end, saying they didn't even know that "old" people did such things!

I am going to have this love baby, and the kids can't wait. Seven built-in baby sitters! My husband continues to be in shock (six weeks later) and is the brunt of every kind of joke at work.

We got married on horseback, and had twelve horses in the wedding party. The judge came riding up to take his place in the front to marry us. As he was riding up the hill to his position, he hit his head on a branch from a tree and fell off the horse. He started to bleed and he was a mess.

He took it in stride, regained his composure, and married us while holding a napkin to his bleeding head. After the vows, we all trotted off into the sunset to the reception around the side of the barn.

I took her out to a really fancy country club for a romantic candlelight dinner. I had planned the evening by getting us a great table and asking the waiter to put the engagement ring on top of her dessert under a cover. However, when we finished our dinner, she was not in the mood for any dessert. I had to force her to order one, which I said I would share. She finally consented, after I had sweated it out for 15 minutes! The dessert came and I was so nervous that I almost passed out. Anyhow, the waiter put it in front of her and removed the cover, when she saw the ring, she became hysterical, and I became calm. I couldn't stop her from crying and everyone at the restaurant was staring at us. She got up and embraced me and said "yes, yes, yes." It was simply fantastic! After dinner, we walked outside on the golf course.

We had a very young rabbi perform our wedding ceremony. This was only his second wedding he had ever performed. During the ceremony, he passed me the traditional glass of red wine to taste as part of the blessings. As he passed it to me, it slipped out of his hand and spilled down the front of my wedding dress into my bra. His face turned as red as the wine! I made quite a fashion statement with six white cloth napkins stapled to the front of my dress, and was very happy that most of our pictures were taken before the wedding.

My fianceé and I spent $740 taking ballroom dancing lessons in the months before our wedding. We couldn't wait to show all of our friends that we could actually dance together. The time was finally here for our very first dance as husband and wife. Nervous would be an understatement. As we walked onto the dance floor, my husband slipped on my wedding gown and would you believe it? He banged his head! But more incredibly, he broke his leg. He spent the rest of the wedding reception sitting with his leg elevated on a chair and lots of ice and a bottle of Tylenol.

My fianceé was eight months pregnant, and we were on our way to the wedding when she went into hard labor. We turned around and went to the hospital. I used my cell phone to call one of my friends who was at the church waiting for us and told him that we would not be making it to the church on time, rather we were going to the hospital to have a baby. We were married in her hospital room about thirty minutes after she gave birth to our new daughter.

Talk about being surprised...when I proposed to my wife, I had set it up beautifully. We went to the circus, and I made sure we had seats in row three. Well, the circus started, and the clowns came out and started to pick people randomly from the audience. They picked my soon-to-be-wife, and dragged her out along with about ten other people, young, old, men and women. The ten of them rode on various forms of clown transportation around the ring. After a few minutes, with all the participants now hysterically laughing, they came back to get more people and selected me. Now they were parading all of us around and around until they started doing funny things with balloons and signs and making little children laugh. Then, for one brief moment, everything stopped and a clown came running out with a

103

sign and he went in front of my lady and turned the sign around to her and it said WILL YOU MARRY ME? She took a moment or two to understand what was going on, and then burst into tears of joy. She rushed over to me, kissed me and said yes, the audience went wild! It was prearranged by me, through a friend who worked for the arena.

I went with a girlfriend to visit her brother in jail. While there, I met his cellmate, and it was love at first sight. I visited him often, and after his five-year sentence was over we were finally able to be together and get married. He is everything I ever wanted in a husband: friend, lover and companion. He said he was guilty of his crime, armed robbery, but will never do it again.

When my husband and I got married he was just getting a divorce…and I mean JUST! I went with him to get his final papers. We then walked next door and got married within five minutes. I had our baby the next day.

I was best friends with my husband's uncle. His uncle and I never dated, but we did have sex. After one year, I moved in with his uncle (just friends and sex). I fell in love with both the uncle and my husband (to be). I got pregnant, and I think the uncle is the father. I am 5 years younger than his uncle and 10 years older than my husband. Now we all live together under one roof. My husband still doesn't know about his uncle and I.

My bachelor party was very wild. The guys took us back to someone's house, where we drank and drank and drank. We watched x-rated movies, and then the guys brought in two strippers. I was blown away when I saw that one of the strippers was my wife's best friend and soon-to-be-maid-ofhonor. She and the other girl grabbed me and took me into another room, where they forced me to have sex with them. It was exciting and terrible at the same time. I was afraid she would tell my wife. A few days later, we had a rehearsal for the wedding, and the girl showed up and whispered to me that she would never tell my wife what happened, but that I was now her sex slave whenever she felt the need. It is terrible. I don't know what to do. I've been married for three months and she shows up at least once a week at my office and forces me to have sex with her. What am I to do?

Note: This is a real story that we received among thousands. It is one of the more amusing stories and true if not, you must admit it is rather unique.

I dated a lot of jerks who were all interested in the same thing in the 16 years following my divorce. About a month before I met my current husband, I was held up at gunpoint, nearly run over by a truck, and had several girlfriends who were dumped by their guys. Needless to say, I was not thrilled with men at this time! When I met my husband on a blind date, I was not very trusting, as you can imagine. However, he quickly showed me that there were still a few good men out there. He also made me believe in fairy tales. From day one, he has made me feel very happy. I'm the happiest I've ever been in my entire life!

Both of our spouses passed away, so we attended a bereavement group. We met there and were married after three months. We even have a wonderful sex life at ages 81 and 83! Loved your questions.

My sister was staying with us shortly after we were married. My husband and I were going at it hot and heavy. My husand put on a condom and then decided to take it off. As he was taking it off, his hand slipped, and the condom snapped right into his privates. He screamed, and I laughed so loud that my sister burst into the room to see what was going on and saw us in this very compromising position. My husband's pain turned to embarassment. He just about died!

My husband and I had the most unusual and outrageously sad and funny incident happen all at once to us about two months ago. Just married three months, we were very much still on our honeymoon, very much in love, and having lots and lots of great sex. We enjoyed being alone in our town-house with a beautiful bedroom upstairs, and the living and dining rooms on the lower level.

My husband's brother and three of his college buddies de-cided to come and stay with us for ten days on spring break. It was fun to have them stay and they were no bother; they slept downstairs on the couch and floor. They were basi-cally really nice young guys.

Early one evening the guys said, "We are going out to rent some movies and have dinner," and asked if we wanted to go with them. We declined. As soon as they left, we went upstairs to our bedroom and got into a very heavy, wonder-ful sexy mood.

As we were making love, and I need to tell you that we were both naked and I (female) was on top, there was a quick knock on the bedroom door and his brother said," Hi! We're back." I immediately said, "Don't come in yet," but he opened the door. It was as if time stood still. There he was, standing absolutely frozen. It seemed like hours, but it was probably ten seconds before he closed the door and ran downstairs.

I was devasted, more concerned for him than for me. He was only a boy, 18 I think. I broke down crying and asked my husband what to do. "Your baby brother is probably so humiliated, he won't ever face me, talk to me, or have anything to do with me. What am I supposed to do? The poor kid will probably be ruined for life." My husband calmed me down, and we decided that the best plan would be for me to go downstairs (where he probably was laughing with his buddies about what happened) and break the ice by saying something funny, like "Well, I guess you know that your brother is not a virgin anymore." A silly statement, but I hoped it would clear the air...

I waited about half an hour, got dressed, and went downstairs. As I got to the last two steps, I realized I was petrified and it was very quiet. I was preparing my funny speech, when I saw the four guys sitting on our couch, reading newspapers. As soon as I took my last step and reached the living room, the four of them stood up and dropped the newspapers, they were stark naked and laughing aloud. I was so shocked I couldn't breathe! We all began to laugh. My husband rushed down the stairs to see what the commotion was, and he nearly fainted.

It turned out that the fears of my brother-in-law and I were the same. We both thought we would never forget what had happened, but we quickly broke the ice and had a tremendous laugh about it.

# Sometimes what they didn't tell us is as interesting as what they did tell us!

How do I do that? Well, in reviewing the questionnaires, I took a look at the unanswered questions to find out what they didn't tell us. What makes this so interesting is that the following are the percentage of newlyweds that DID NOT answer specific questions. It doesn't make any sense because we did not collect the names of any of our respondents. They had no reason not to answer a question. Read it and see if you can figure it out...

| |
|---|
| 29 percent did not answer whether they kissed and/or slept together on their first date. |
| 1 percent could not remember the first time they slept together. |
| 6 percent could not remember how long they had dated before they had sex for the first time. |
| 8 percent wouldn't tell us how many times they made love on their honeymoon. |
| 7 percent wouldn't tell us if they had sex before they were married. |
| 10 percent clammed up as to who controlled the remote for the TV. |
| 6 percent wouldn't divulge who took care of the money. |
| 4 percent couldn't remember if they had asked their partner to change his/her lovemaking techniques. |
| 5 percent couldn't rememberhow often they had sex before marriage. |
| 13 percent wouldn't tell us how often they had sex in the last month. |

# About the Authors

For Barry Sinrod this is his seventh book. Barry is a product of the 1950's in Brooklyn New York. Coney Island was home back then and Barry attributes his sense of humor and all the good that has come his way to the fact that he was born in Brooklyn.

Brooklyn has produced an enormous number of famous and very talented people.

Barry and his wife Shelly have been married for nearly forty years. They now reside in Florida, after retiring 10 years ago after spending their entire lives in the New York area.

Marlo is new to authoring. She enjoyed co-authoring with her "almost famous" dad. She hopes to continue writing more books down the road! Outside of writing, Marlo's own creations include: three fabulous children, a wonderful marriage, and a successful career in healthcare. What more could a girl ask for?